EXTREME DOT PUZZLES WITH OVER 15000 DOTS

DOT TO DOT PUZZLE

BY **MODERN PUZZLES PRESS**

WILDLIFE ANIMALS

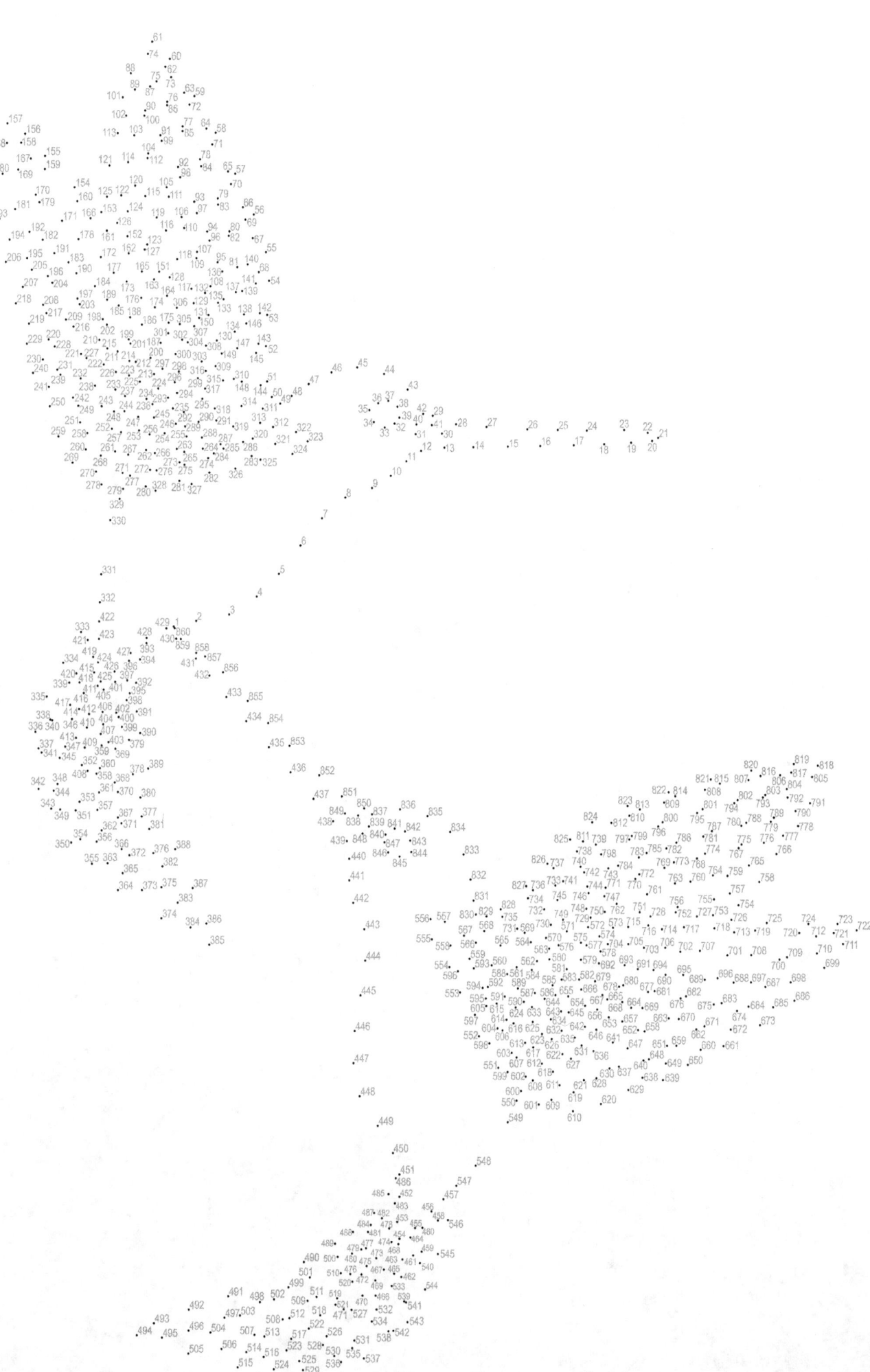

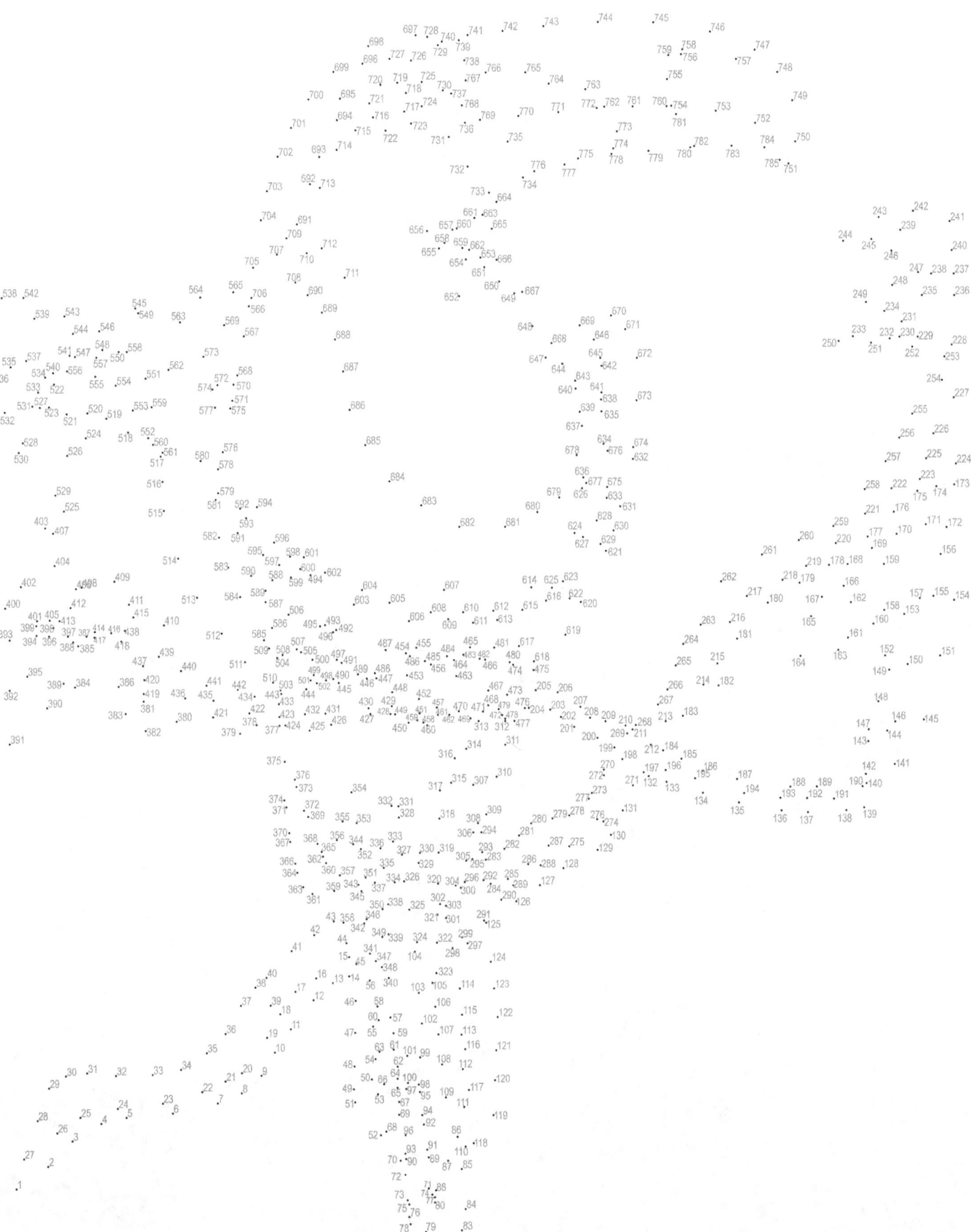

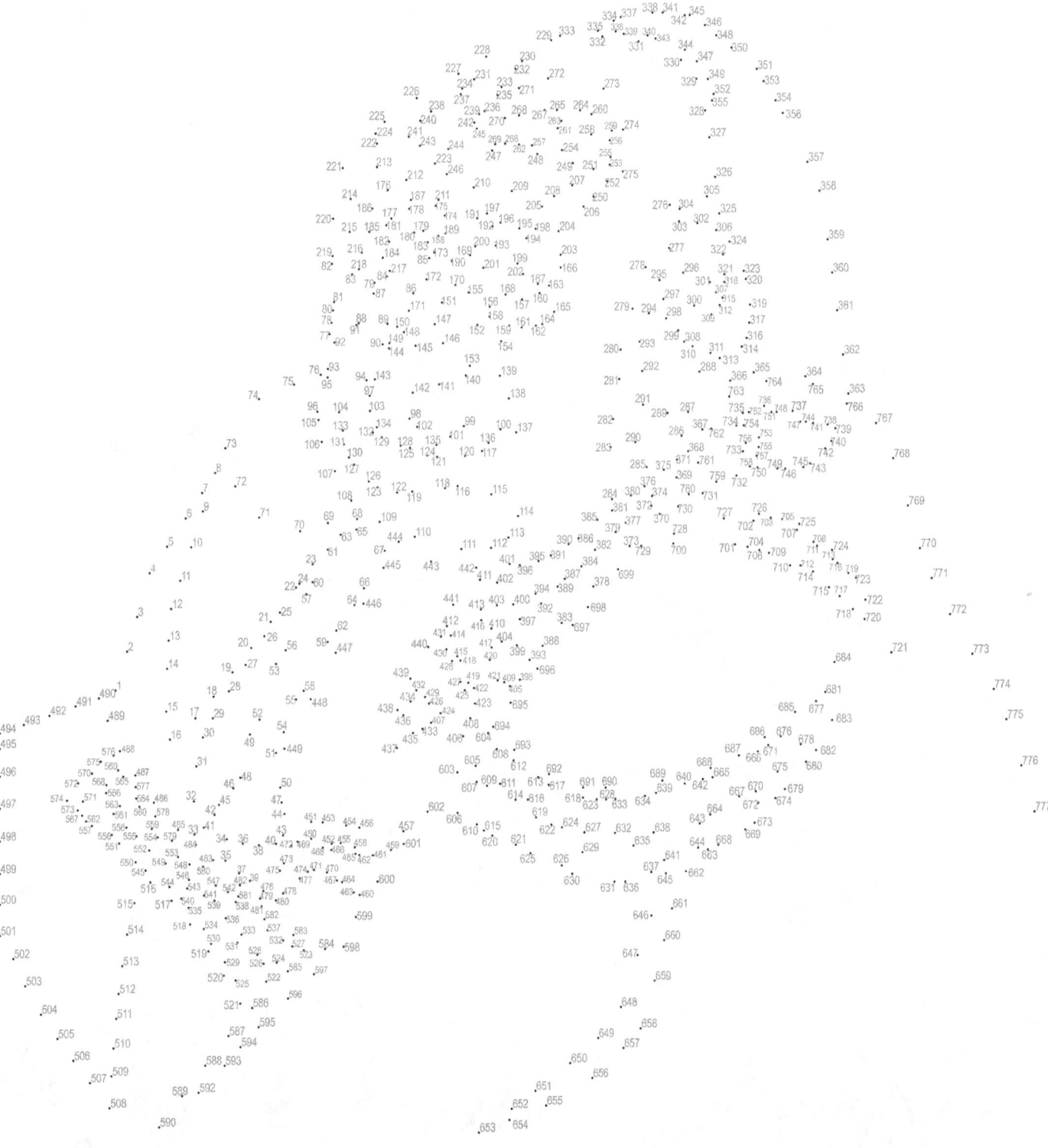

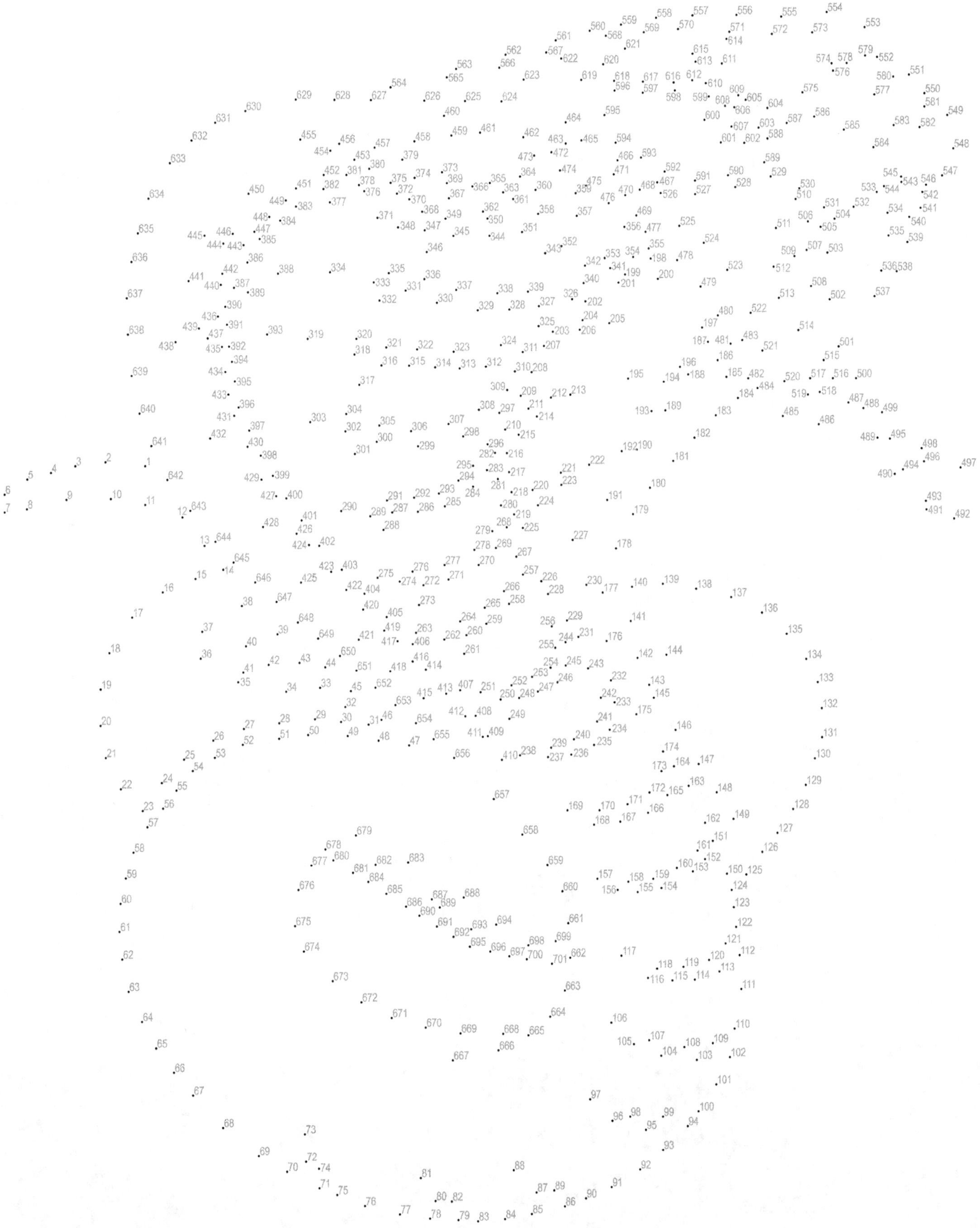

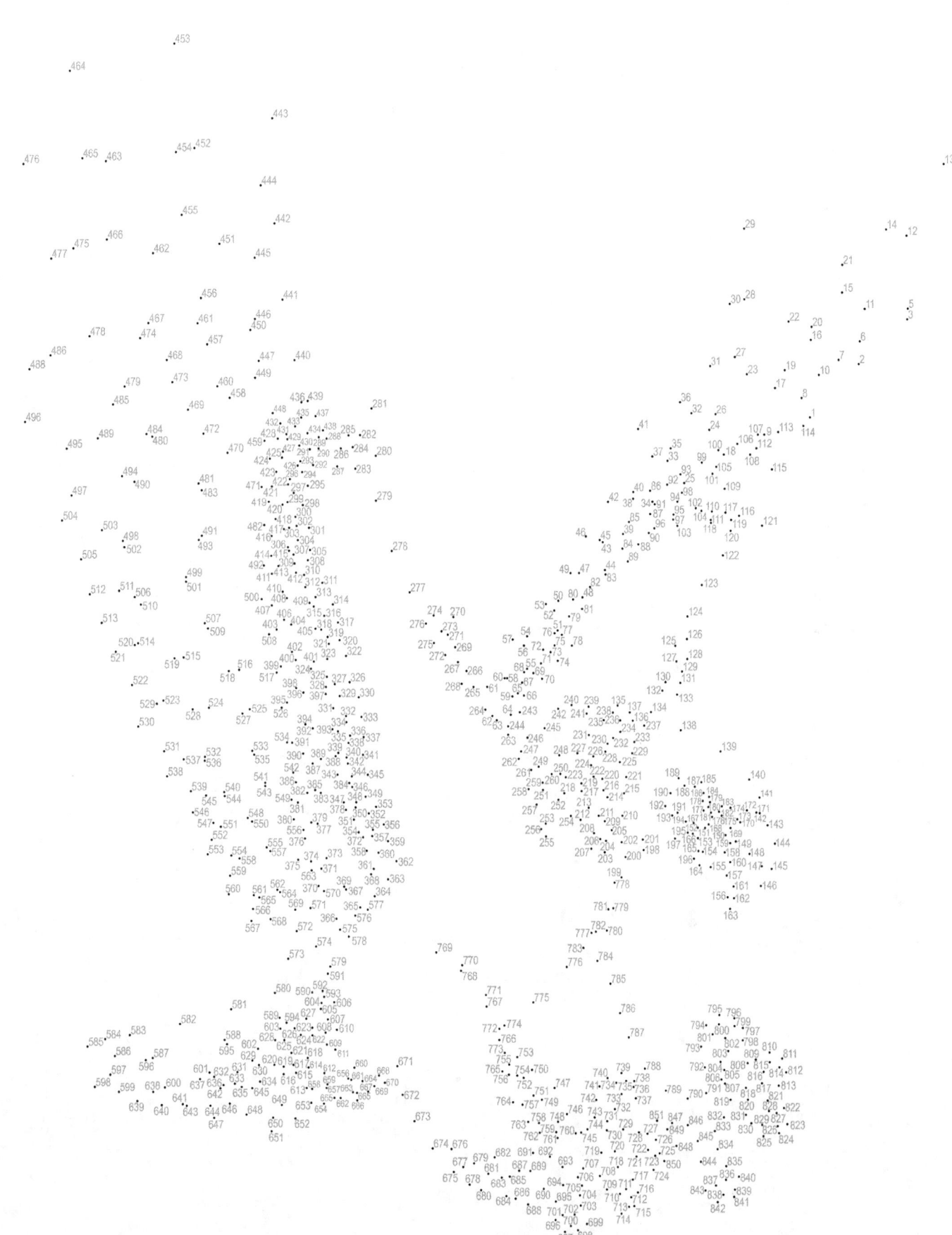

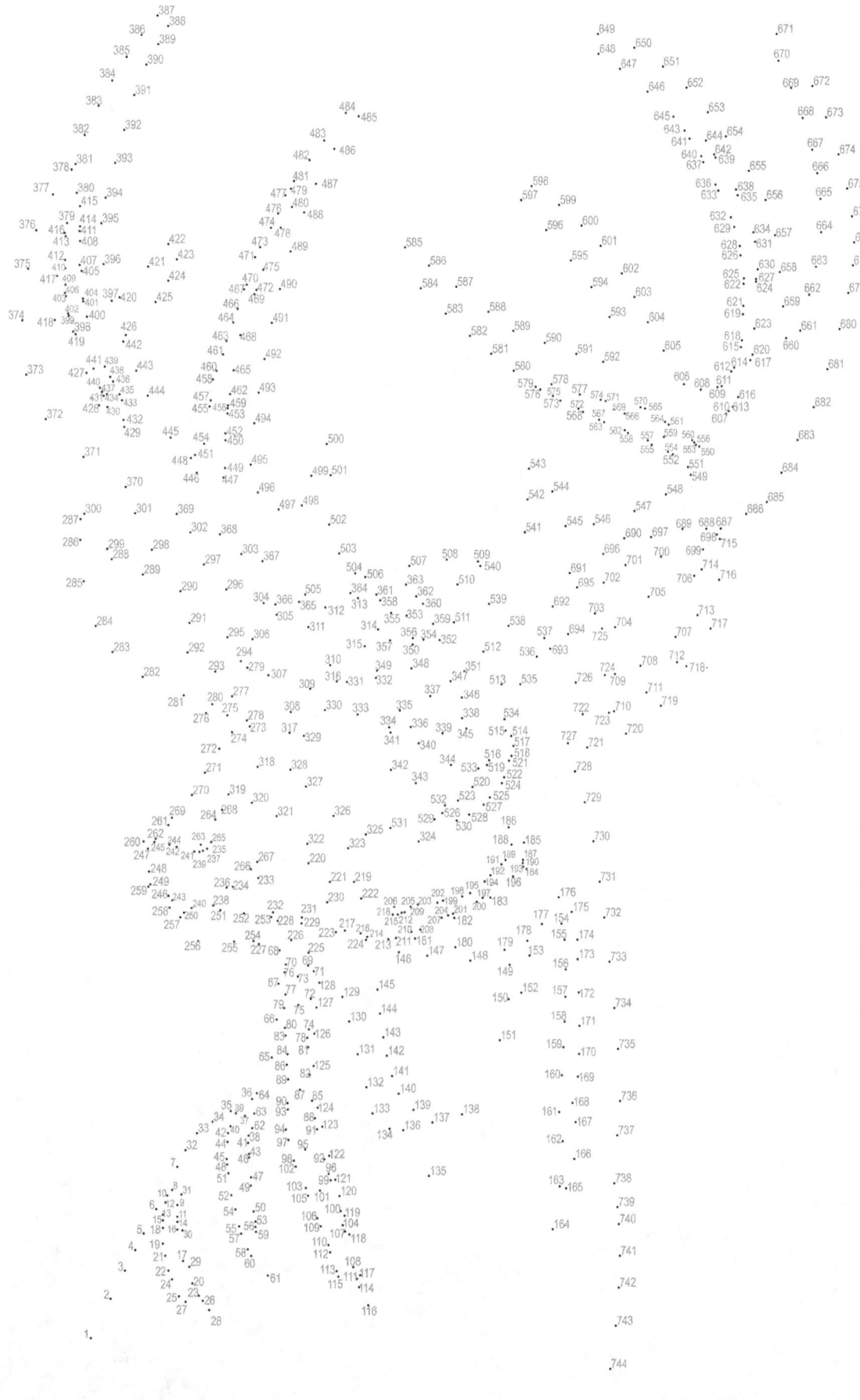

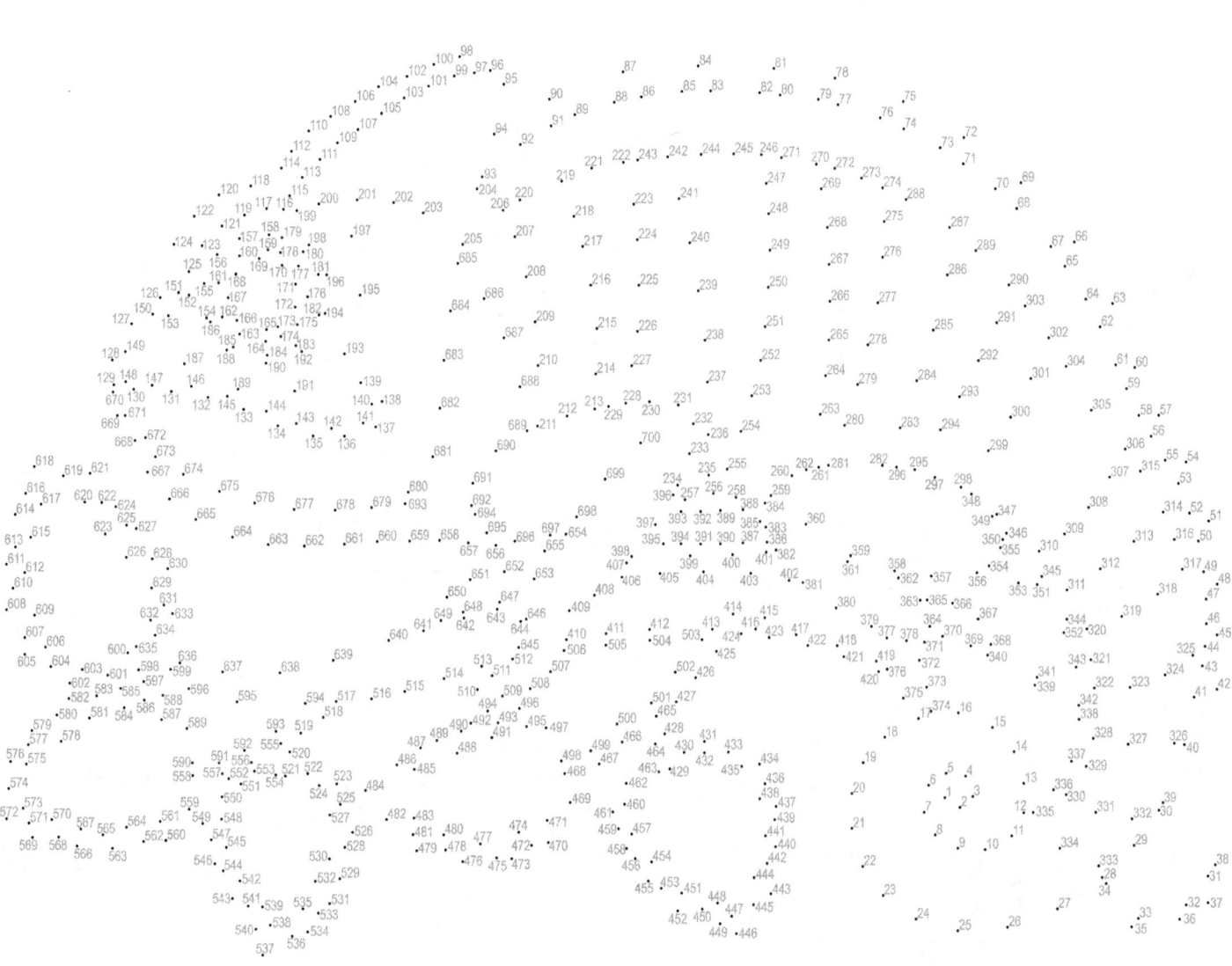

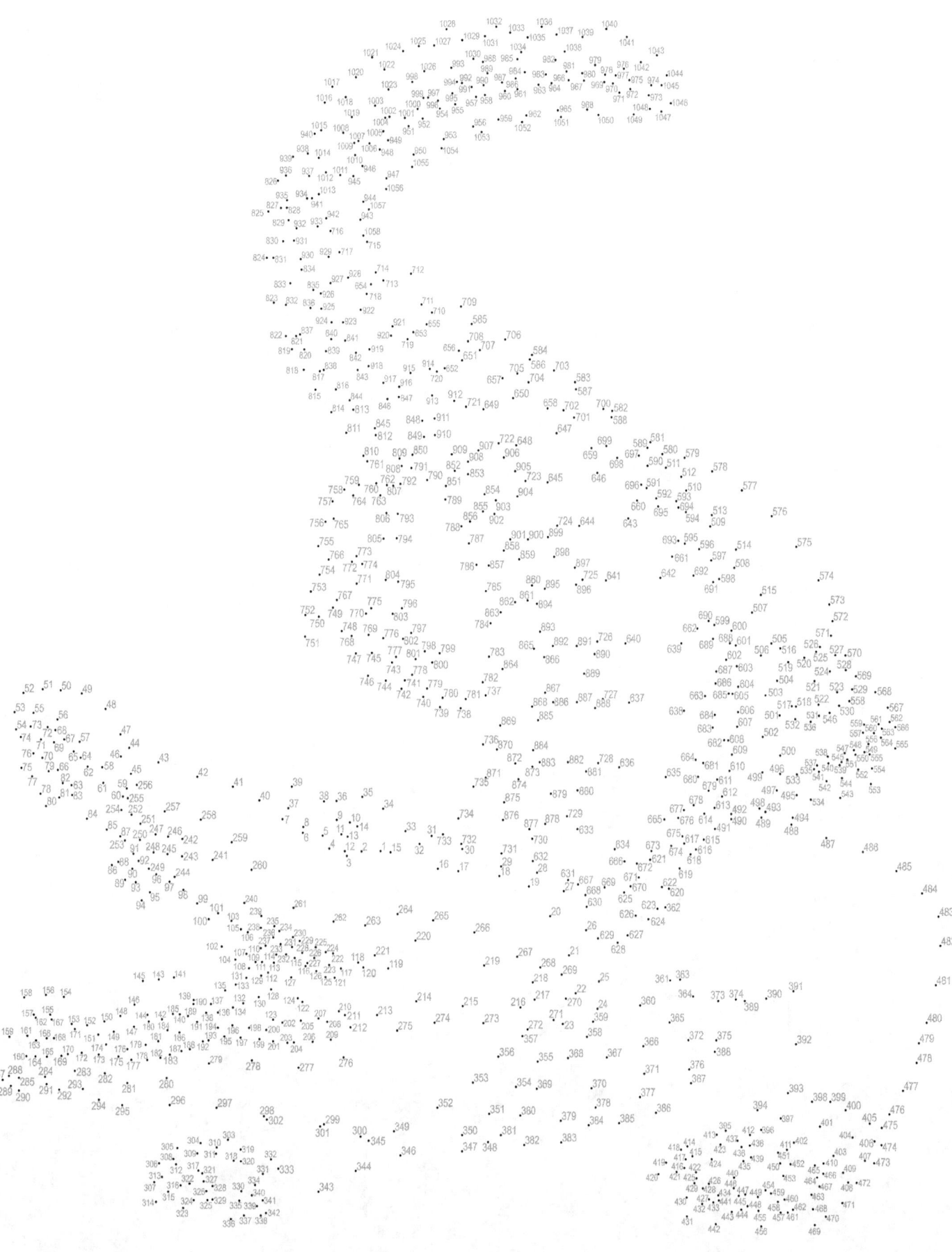

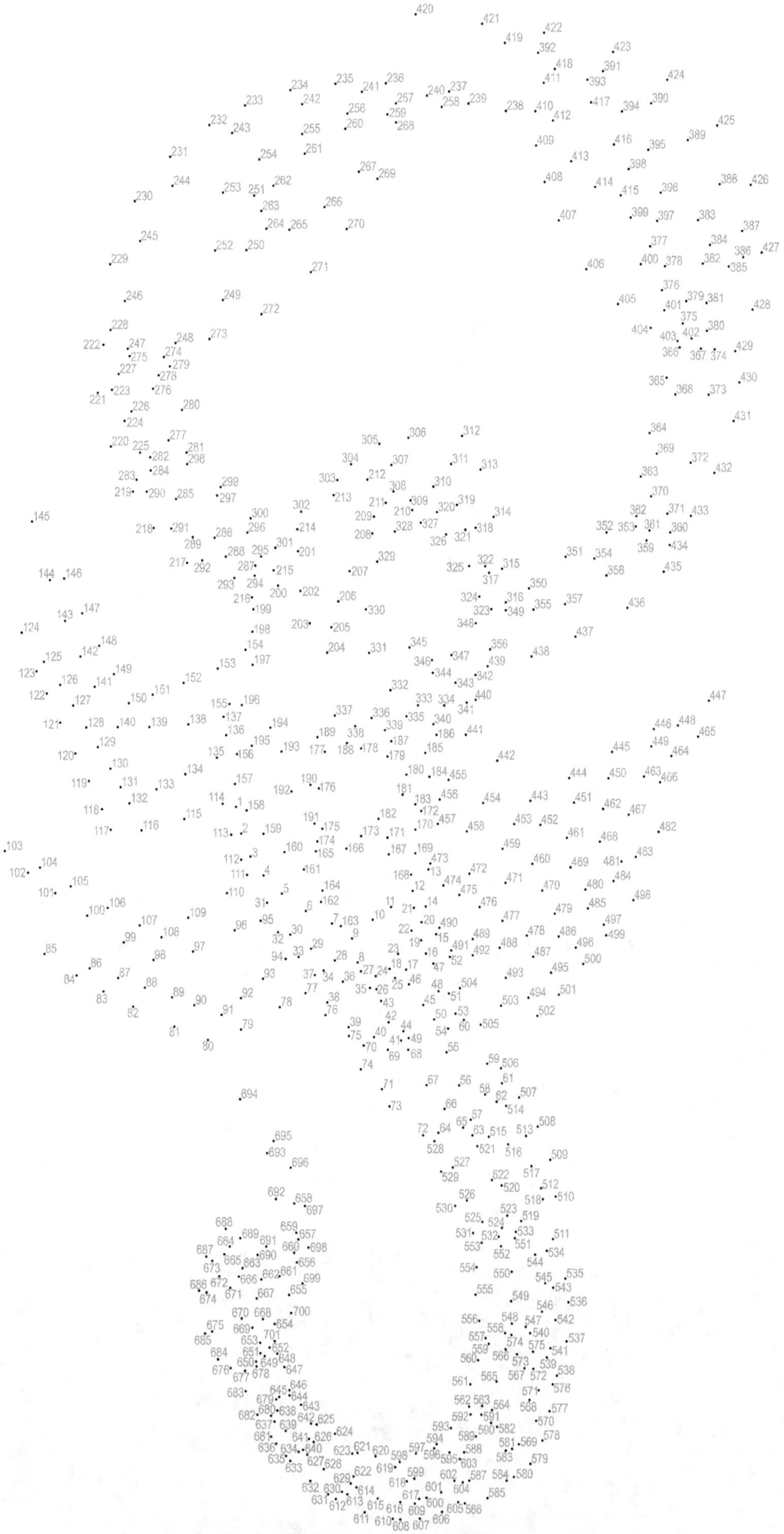

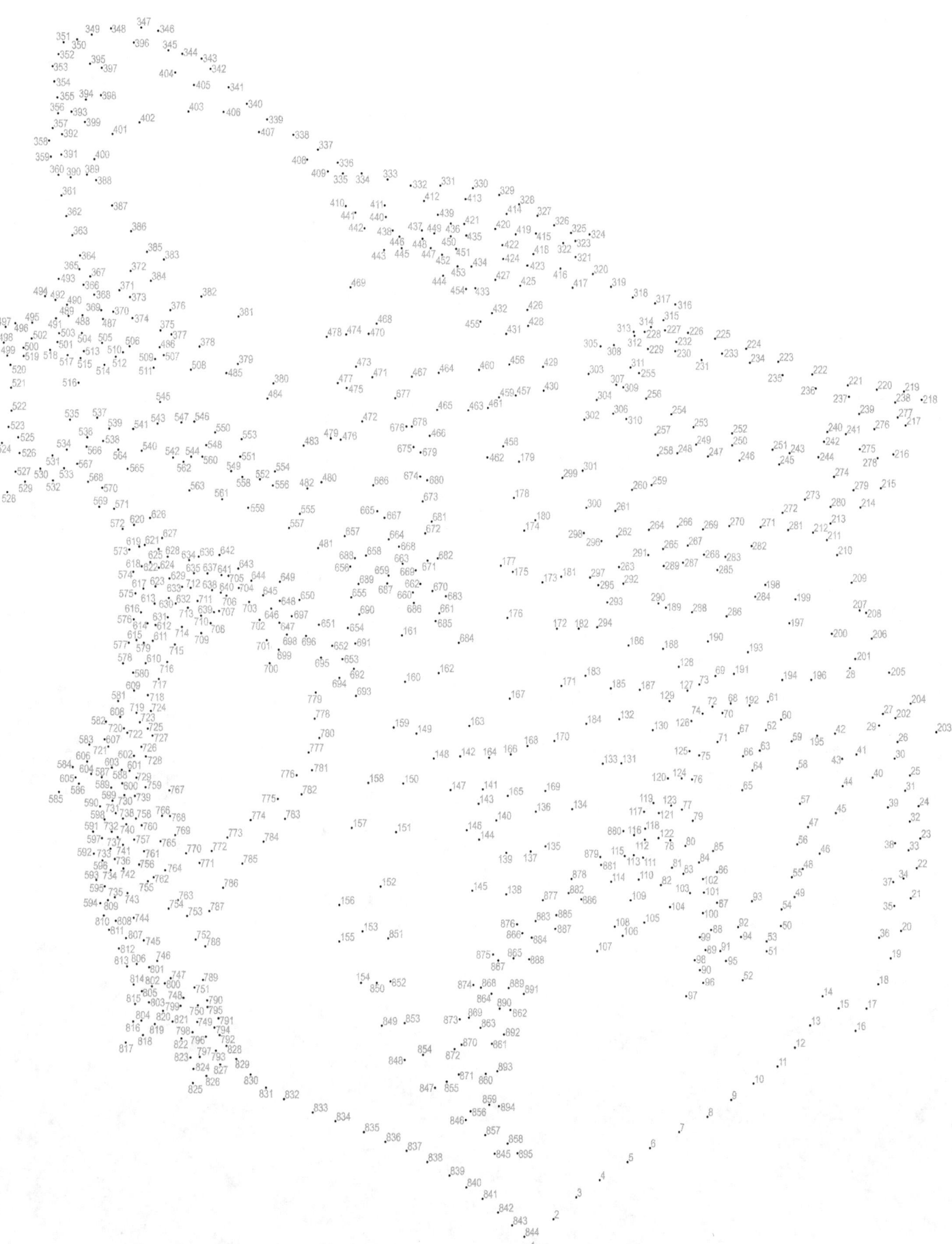

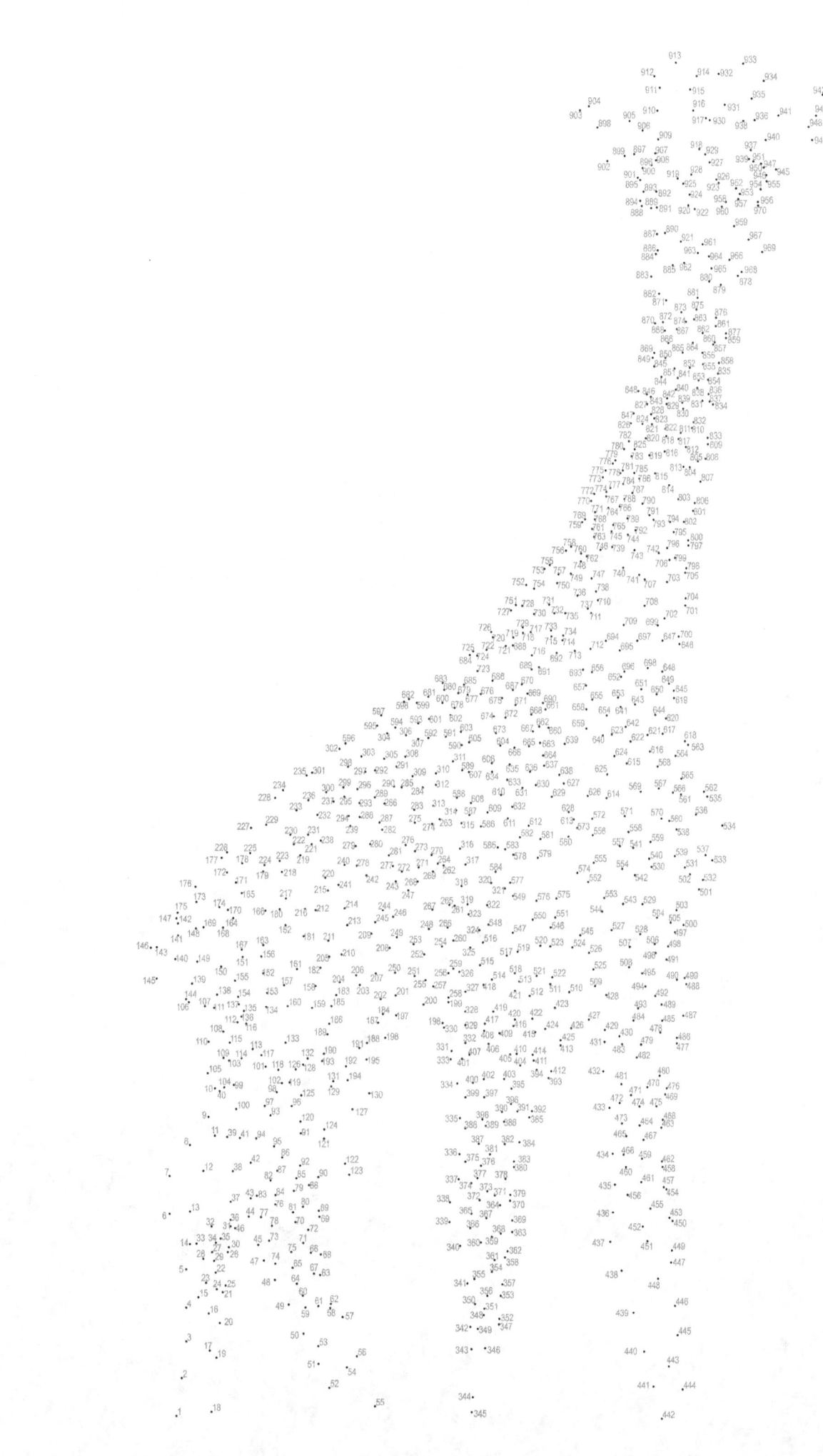

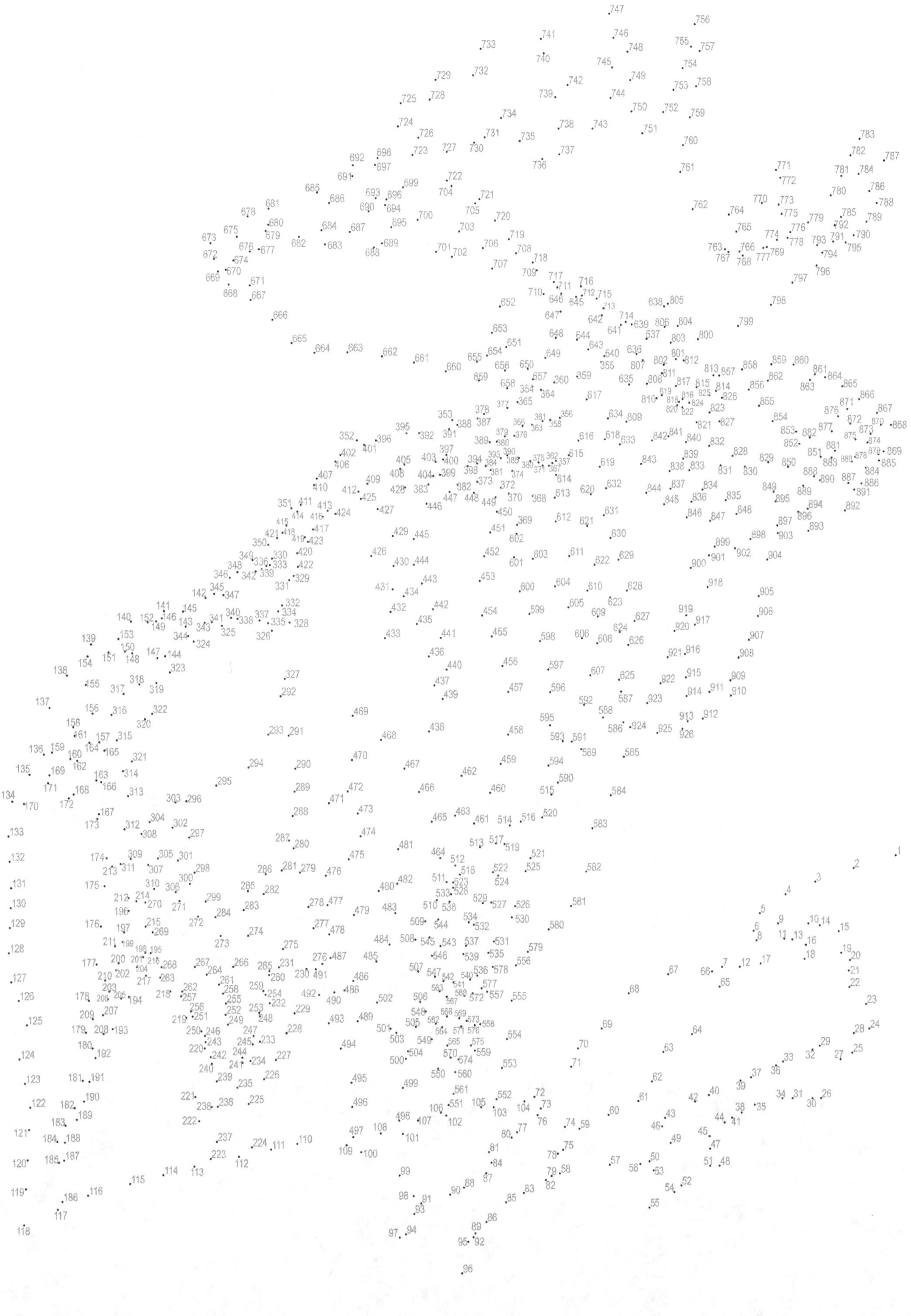

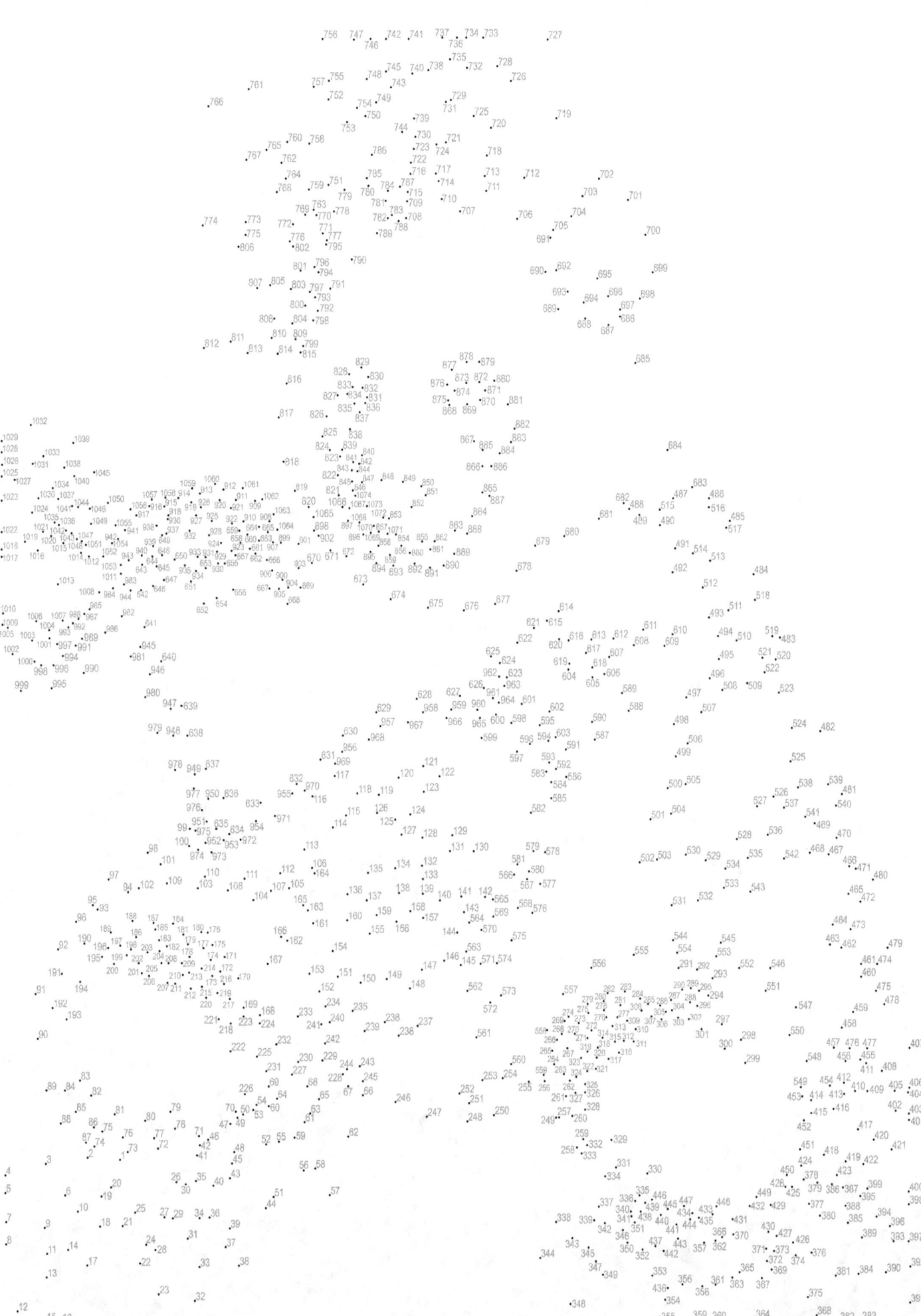

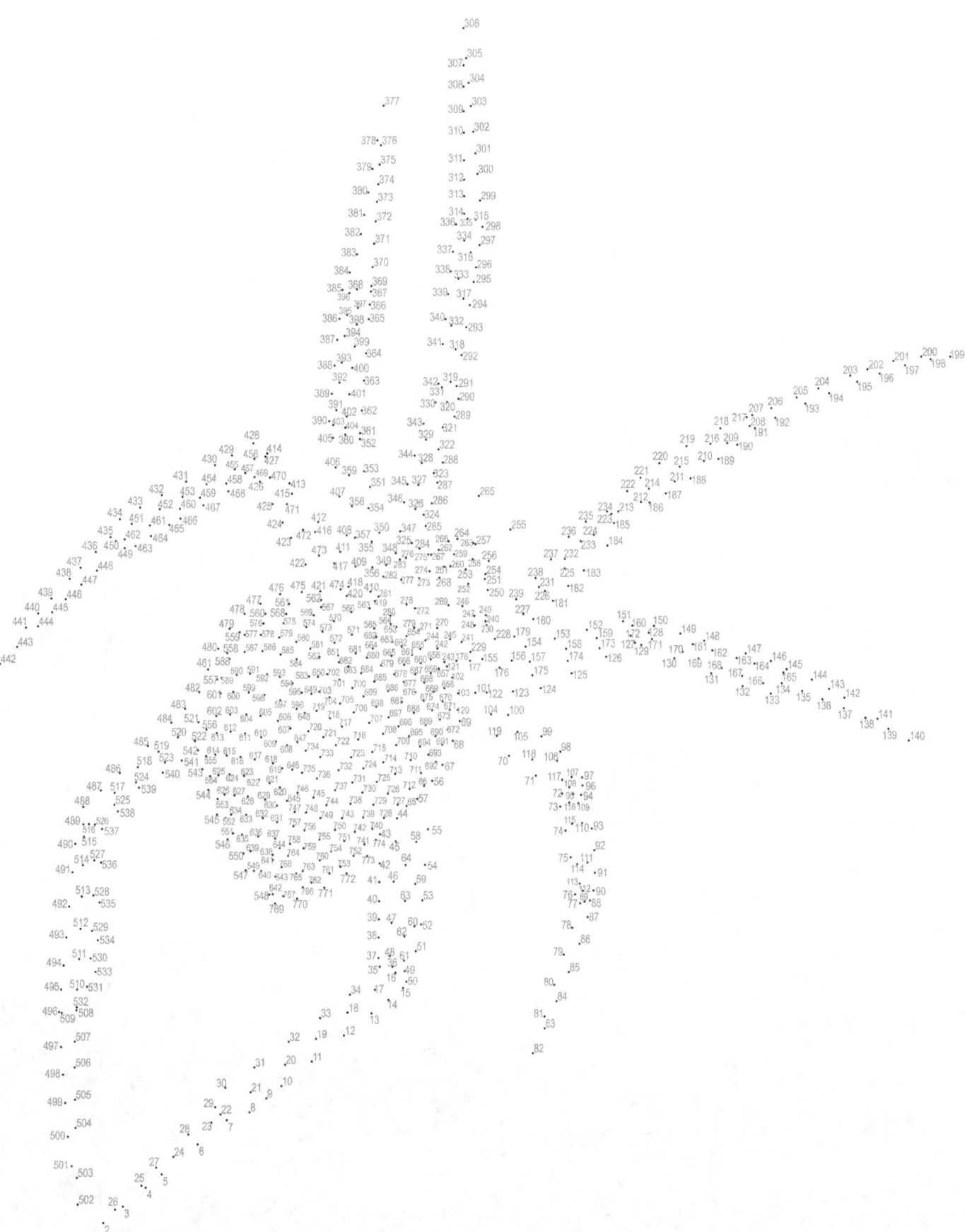

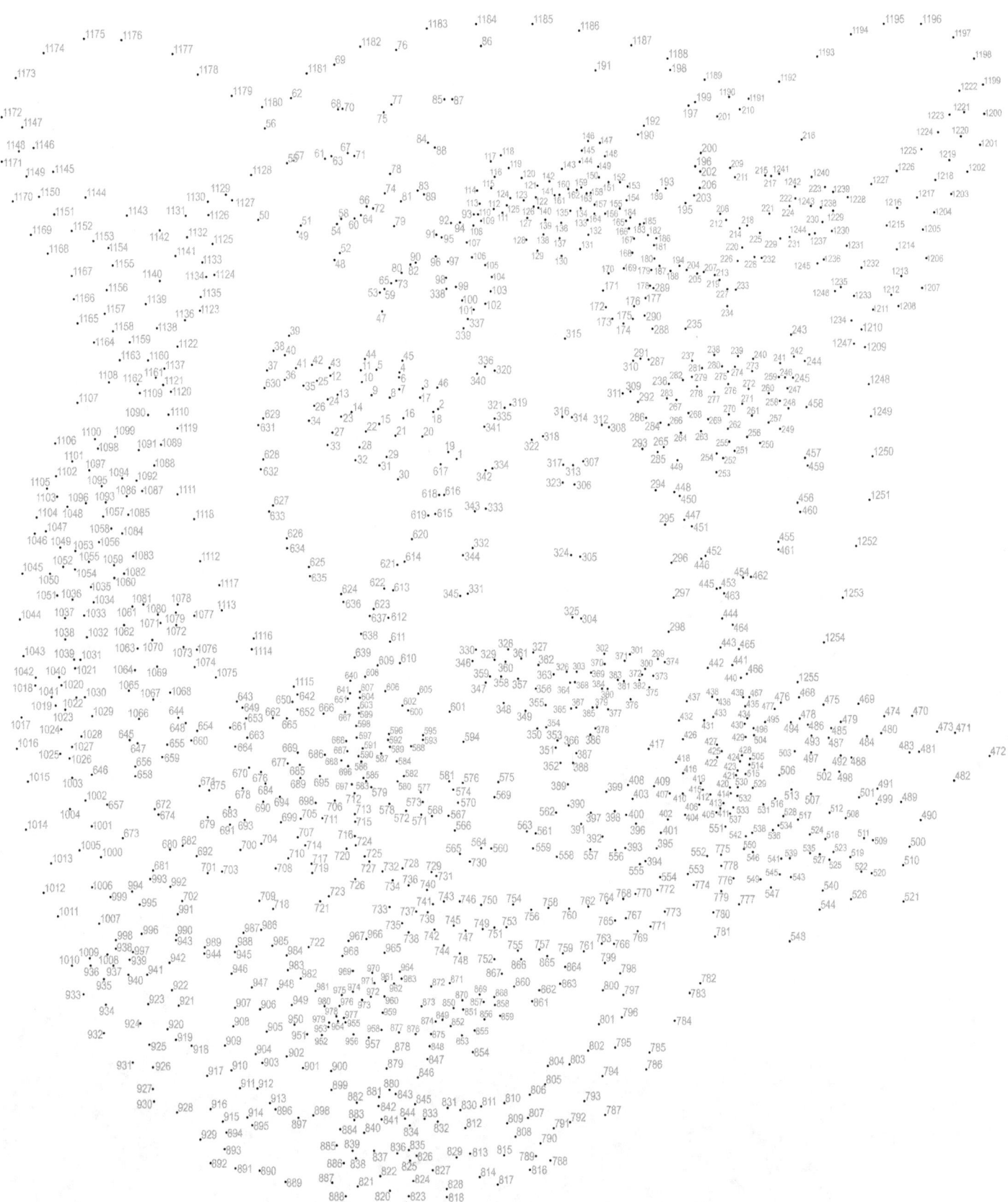

SOLUTIONS

Page 3: Hummingbird

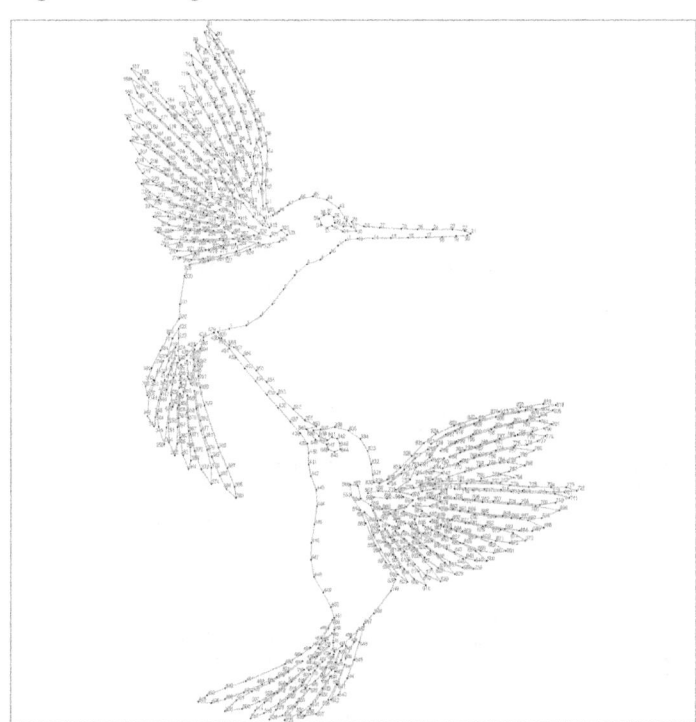

Page 5: Toucan

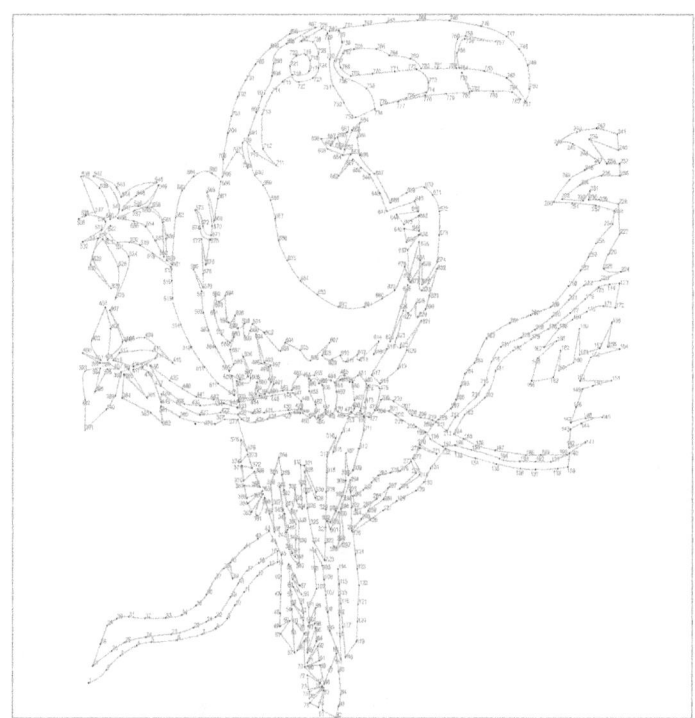

Page 7: Gorilla

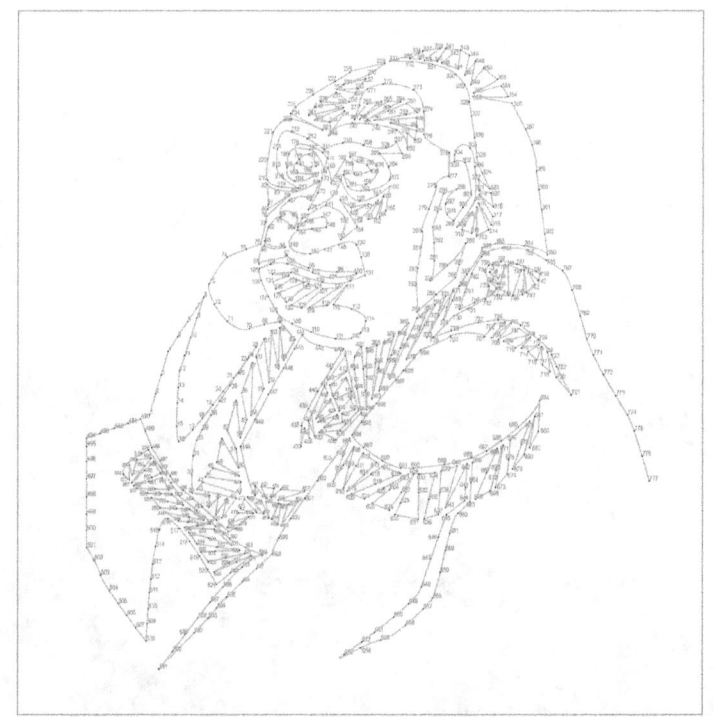

Page 9: Cobra

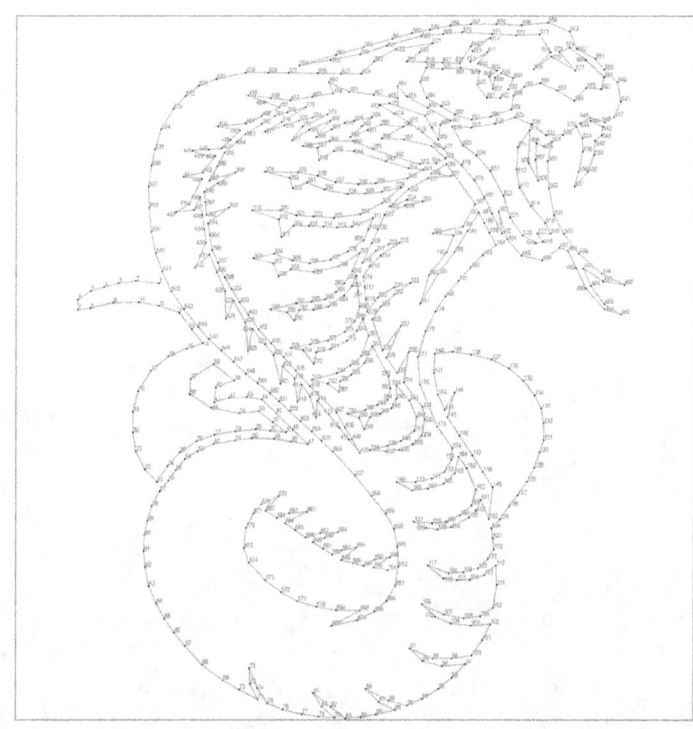

SOLUTIONS

Page 11: Koala

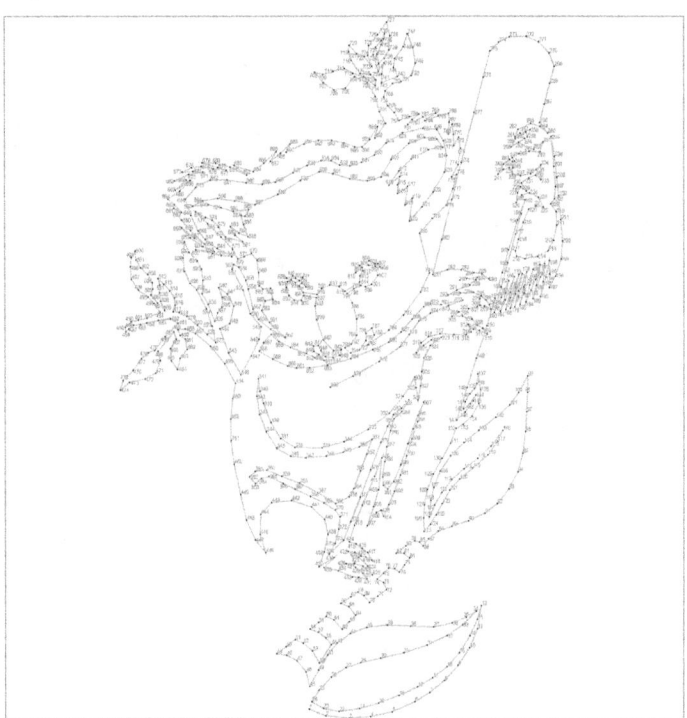

Page 13: Bald Eagle

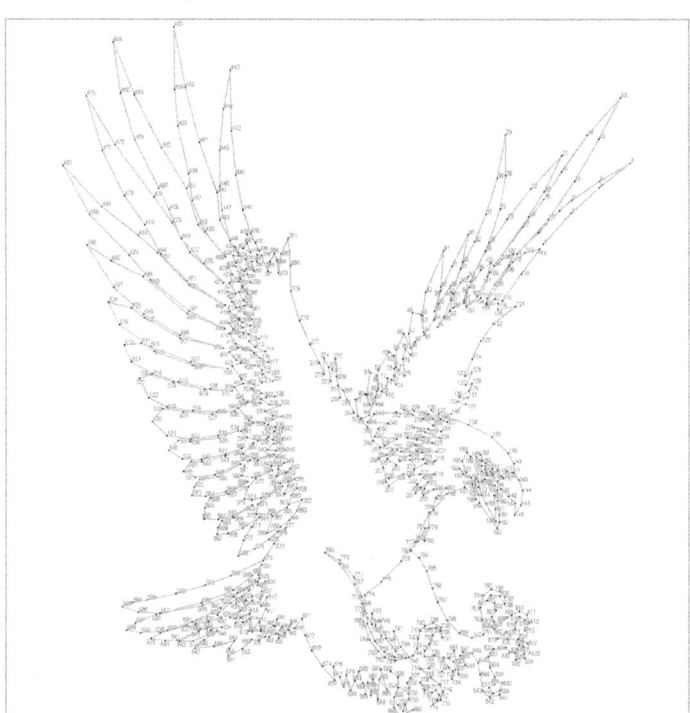

Page 15: Orangutan

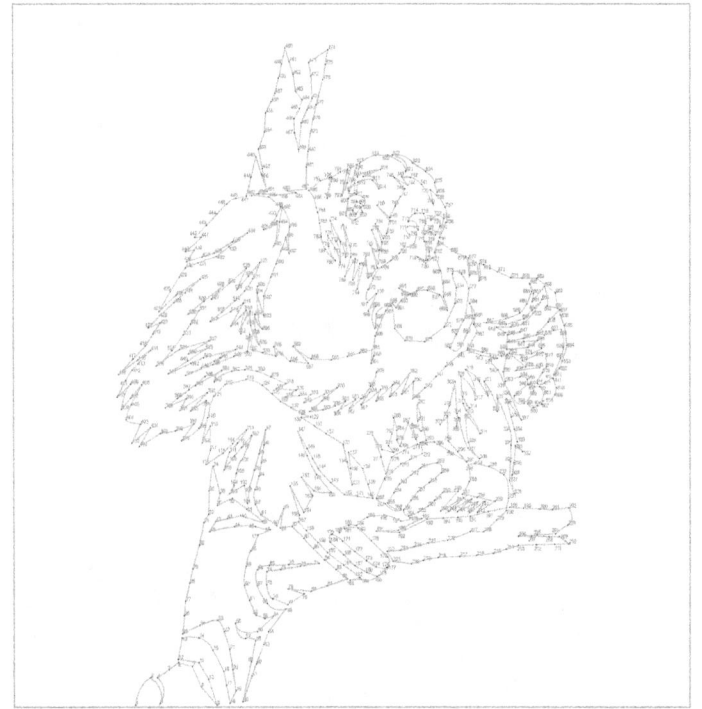

Page 17: Deer

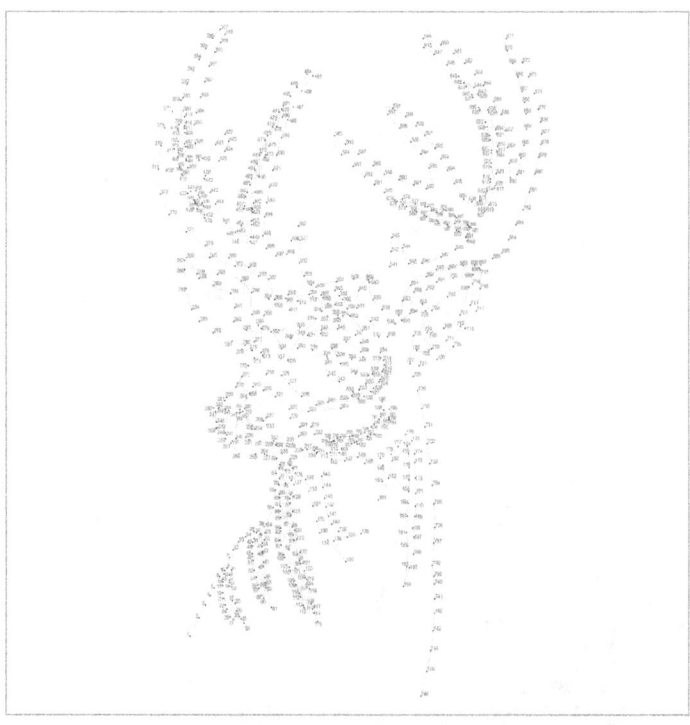

SOLUTIONS

Page 19: Chameleon

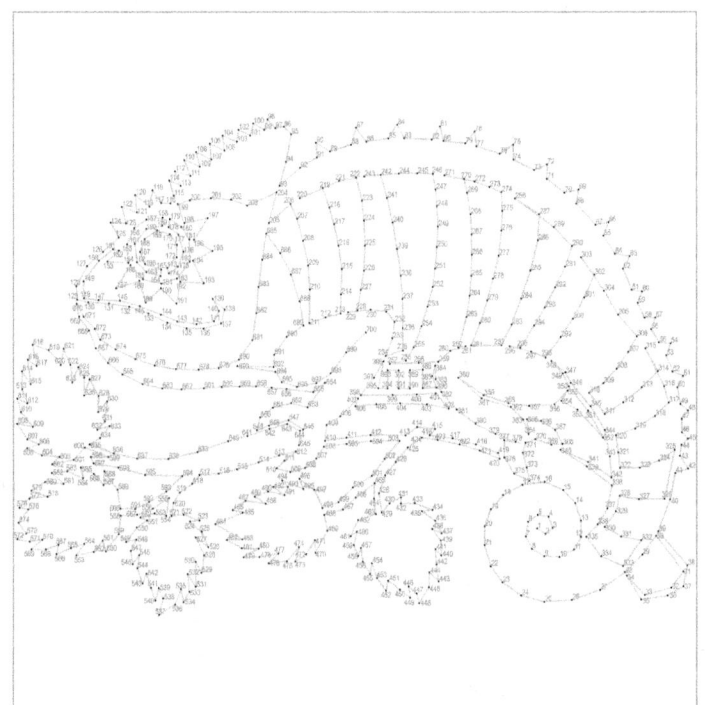

Page 21: Elephant

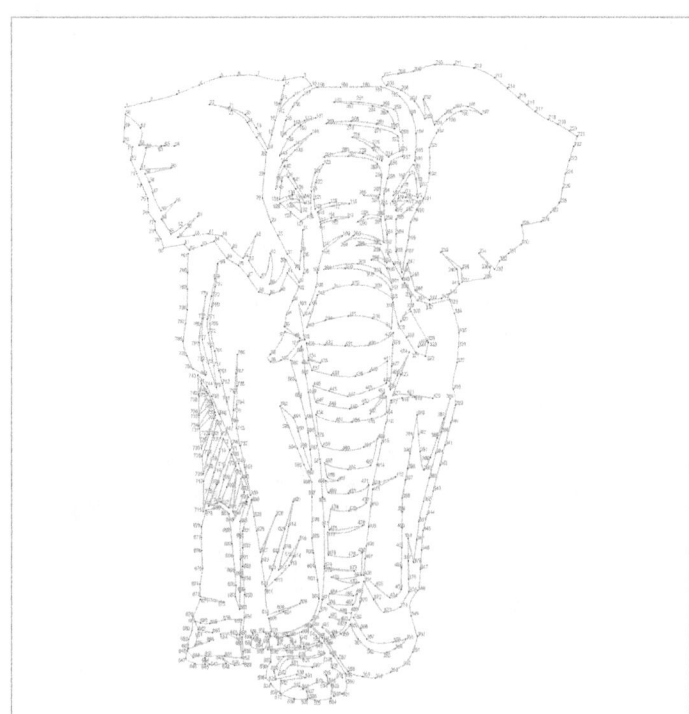

Page 23: Crocodile / Alligator

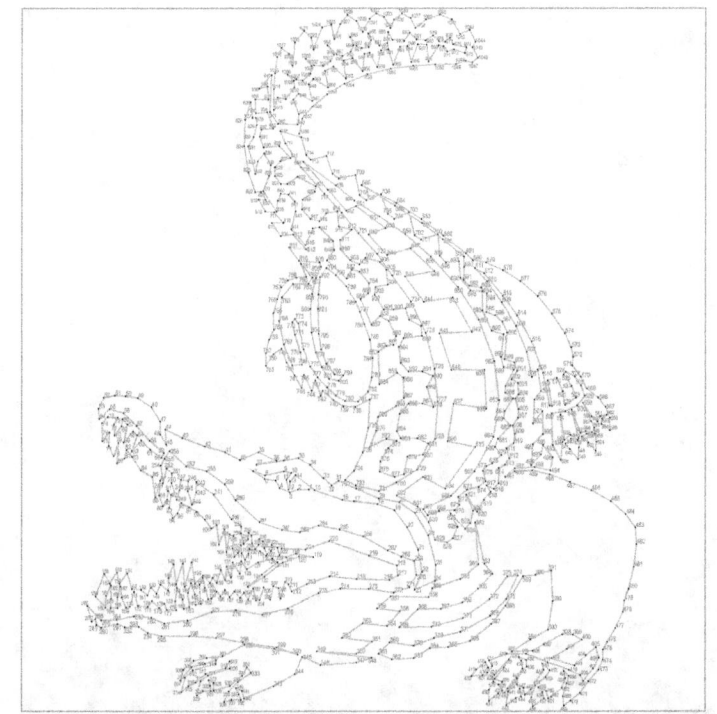

Page 25: Scorpion

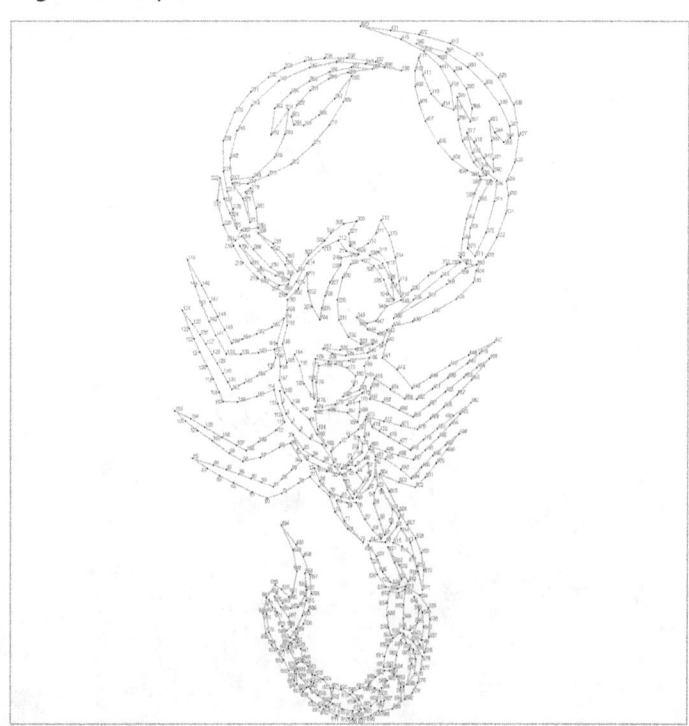

SOLUTIONS

Page 27: Wolf

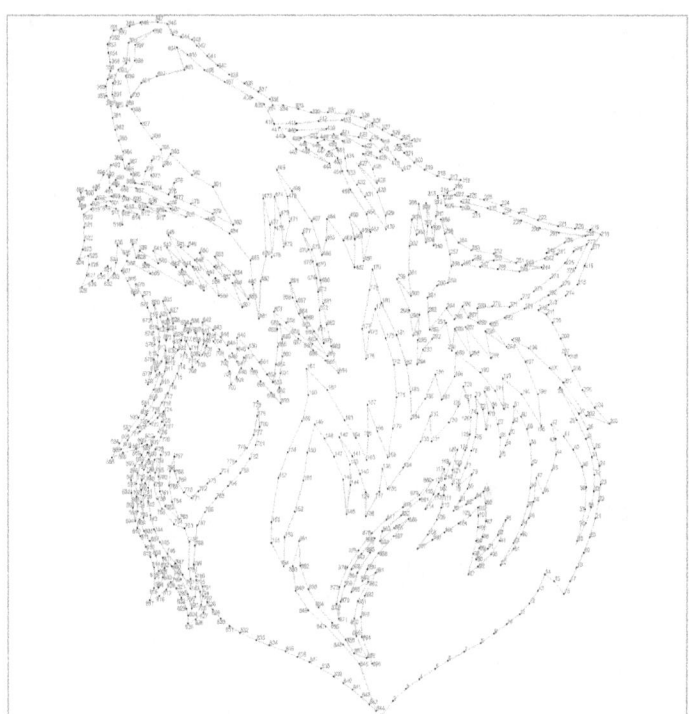

Page 29: Rhinoceros

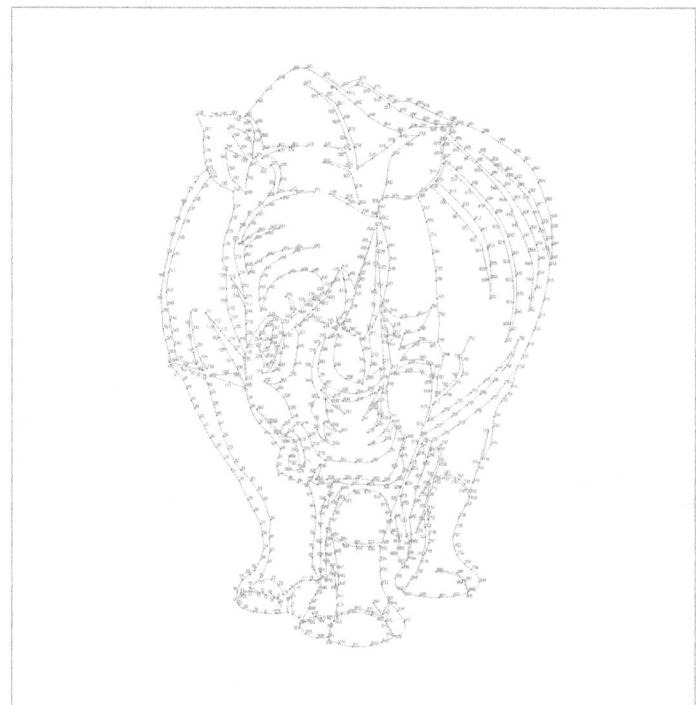

Page 31: Giraffe

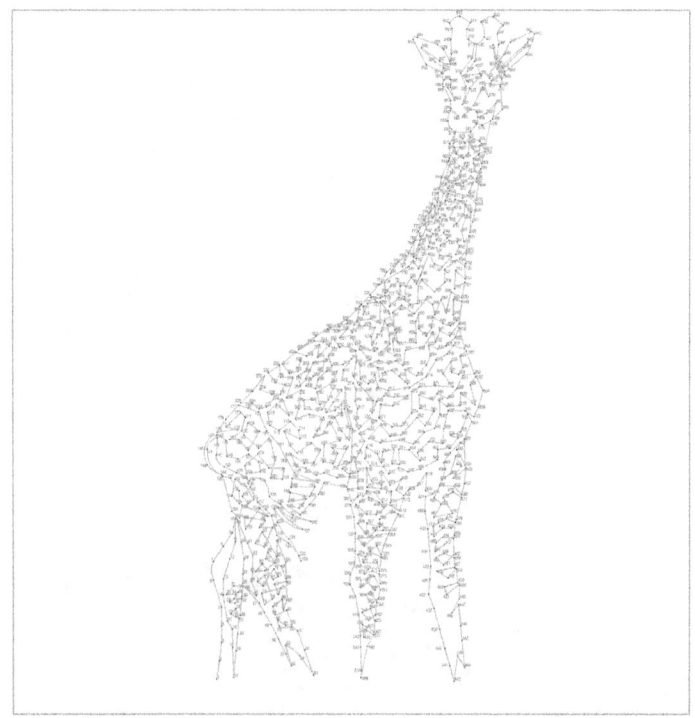

Page 33: Moose

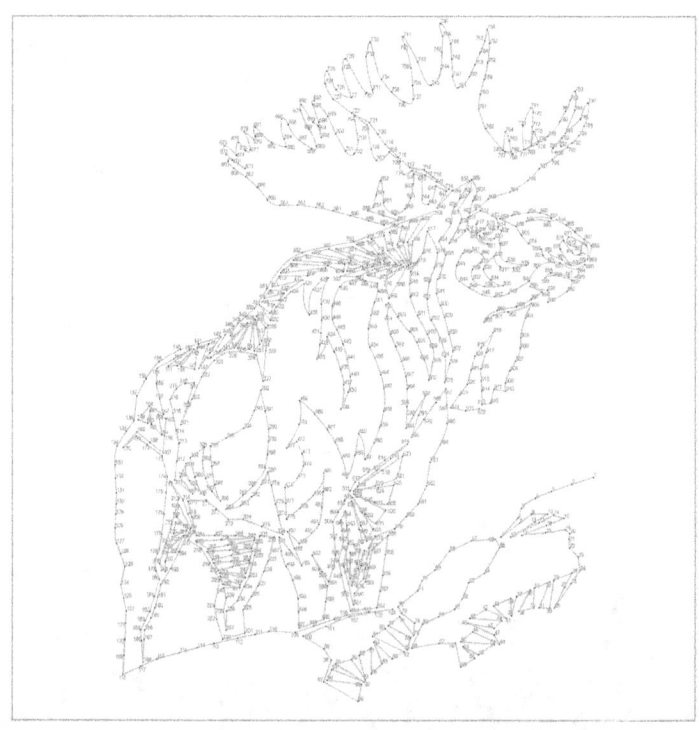

SOLUTIONS

Page 35: Panda

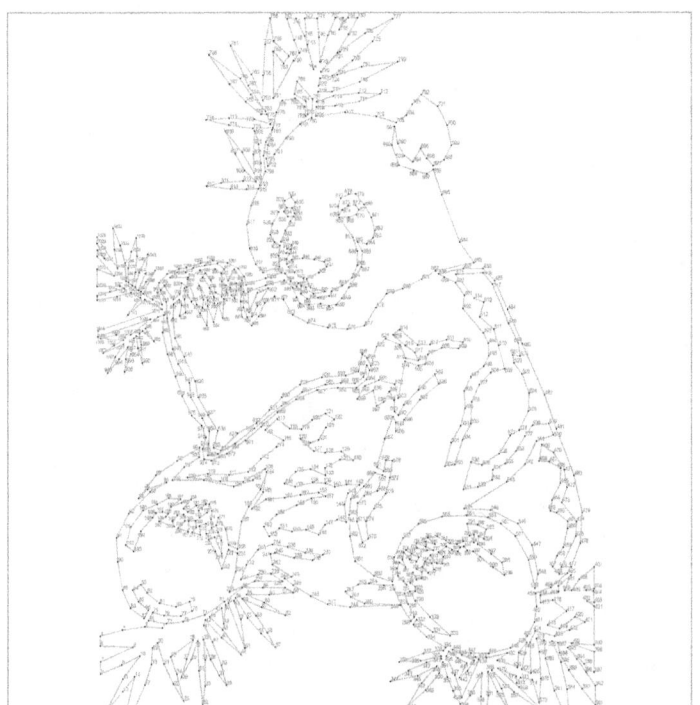

Page 37: Boa Constrictor

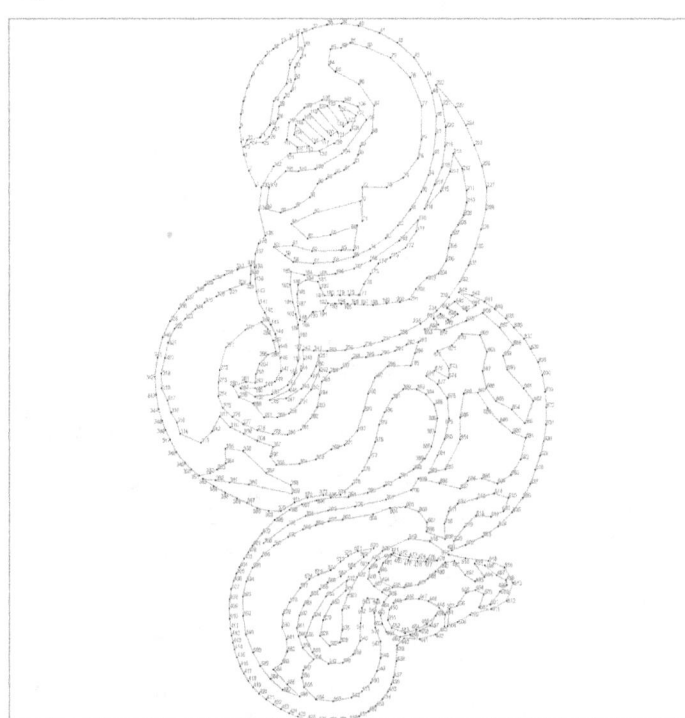

Page 39: Spider

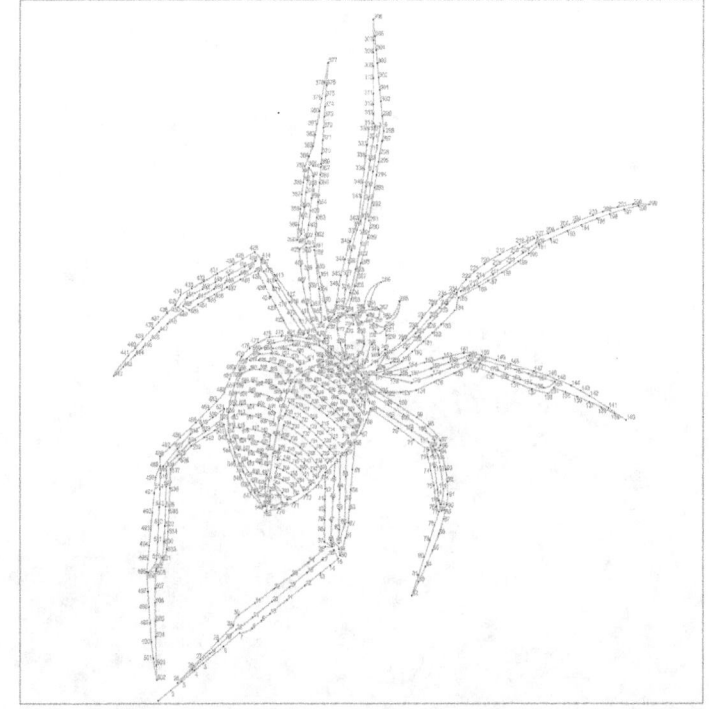

Page 41: Leopard

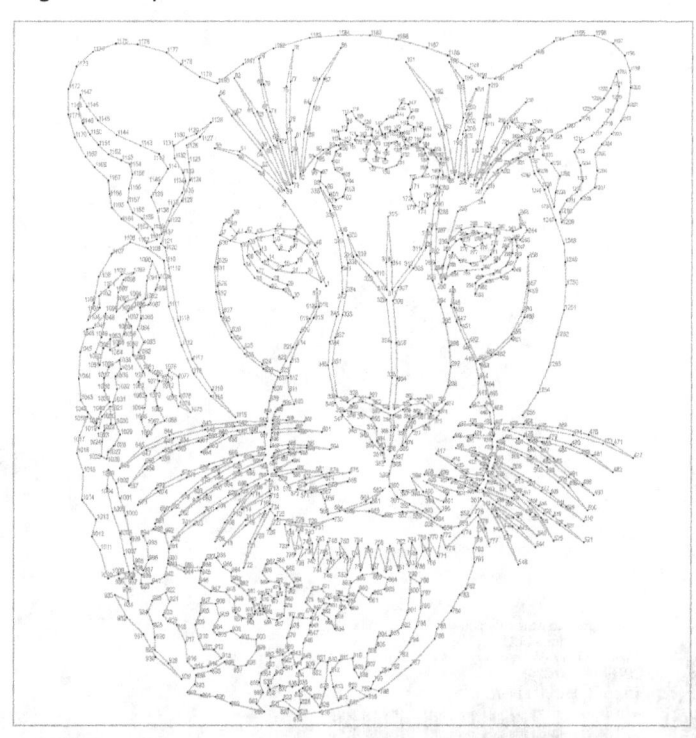